March 11th, 2018 was a collection of mom[...]
me for the better. That was the day I bec[...]
graduate school for a Masters in Teachin[...]
of this one," crept into my mind. Three m[...]
away. Two weeks later, with 80% of my life in the car, it was stolen. The culmination of
events and perceptions out of my control that left me feeling as if I was just in a 12 round
fight with Mike Tyson and he knocked me out...for good. I didn't understand it back then
and I bottled it up. After my car was stolen, I headed out to Montana on a pre-arranged
trip to see my folks. My dad and I was on the golf course...I couldn't hit a good shot to save
my life. On the 8th hole it all came out. I swung and sliced it right...I proceeded to pound
the club in the ground 4 times and then threw it across the fairway. The pressure and
stress flew away with the 8 iron that I threw and at that moment is when the most
amount of clarity I have ever had came over me. Up to that point I had been through a lot.
Never had I been through a collection of events to this magnitude all at once. Yet, with the
release of that 8 iron was the realization of how strong I am and how strong I am capable
of being at any given time. From that moment, was the true turn around, of getting my life
back on track and overcoming the obstacles that were placed within my journey and had
been placed there for a reason.

Life will always be a roller coaster. The adventure park type feeling is what makes life full
and fulfilling. At the end of the day, as I finished this book I realized I wrote this as a
conversation with myself. A platform with free flowing expression that always leads to
one thing...struggle won't ever break me; just like I truly believe that struggle won't ever
break any of us...only if we let it. I grew up in poverty. I grew up in a household that
worked hard but just couldn't quite get out of the hole we were in. The level of damage
that poverty can reach doesn't show its head in comparison to the lessons learned from
the struggle. I watched my mama cry, my dad beam with exhaustion, my brother become
the protector. The great thing about this book is that it's my perspective but allows the
freedom to create one's own perspective. A blank page follows every quote and
description to allow the opportunity for you to express your own perspective.
It's a written trickle effect that will spark the mind into a new state.

Struggle allows for so much success and impact. It doesn't appear for us to crumble but to
challenge us to grow beyond what we believe we are capable of. I believe this book is me,
not only providing perspective and advice on how to handle struggle, but also putting into
action that same advice. With this book I am taking back control of my life. After being
passed up for a handful of full time teaching positions I am controlling the narrative. I am
the one who is in control of the pen that writes the chapters of my life. I am the one who
is going to use every ounce of struggle and every ounce of strength to not let the world
break me but leave it in a better place than when I arrived. I hope you enjoy this book. I
hope you read it with a hunger to gain perspective. I hope you read it in the event that
your life will always be a roller coaster but that you always have the choice to enjoy the
ride.

Your daily dose of peace is your most valuable possession

Your daily dose of peace will create clarity beyond measure. If you fail to take care of self then you're setting yourself up for a break down, physically - mentally - emotionally. You have to realize you're built for more and in order to tap into that you need to hit the refresh button every day. It will propel you into processing information better which will produce greater insight into solving problems, handling difficult situations, and approaching people who are tough to deal with. Invest in self. Feed your mind resources and information on how to handle tough times and situations. The resources are all around us...Music, books, movies, videos, exercise...Etc. Put yourself in the best position possible to flourish beyond the current moment. Invest in self to trigger a greater impact that will add value every single day.

Change Ya Mindset Change Ya Life

Don't let anyone disrupt or steal your swagger

Swagger is the true core of who you are. It's an incredible piece that often gets off track because of the world we live in, the people we surround ourselves with, and/or our own views of self. Swagger is your attitude, mindset, quiet confidence, the thing people first notice when you walk into a room. Build healthy habits every single day. Stop comparing yourself to others and listening to other people's opinions about you. It's your life and the fear of being judged needs to diminish. Live life with a free mind and watch your swagger open up doors. It will propel you to an abundance of opportunities. Protecting self from people who fail to see YOU fully is the best investment you'll ever make.

The spark we carry triggers the impact

You carry a spark inside. You have such great potential. Often, life or other people, dim that spark and leave us feeling empty. However, your mindset and attitude dictates whether you let life or those people extinguish your spark. Everyday is a chance to show the world your gift. Everyday is a chance to overcome the negativity thrown at you. You're born to let your spark, not only lead the way, but impact the next person. Your spark will trigger impact for generations to come. So, turn on your fog lights to see through the foggy weather that life or others may present in front of you. It's time to tap into everything that you are.

Change Ya Mindset Change Ya Life

Create your own beat...walk to your own music...it's your life. Don't let anybody steal your song

My grandfather was a music lover. He was involved in choir and playing his fiddle. He always had his own rhythm, his own beat to life. How he lived created a fantastic song. His ability to interact and impact was the greatest thing I ever observed. He made everyone feel appreciated and heard...he provided hope. You have your own type of song that is waiting to be created. Once you focus on what you feed yourself, who you surround yourself with and make the choice to fully embrace who you are, then it all begins to come together. It's time to realize what you can bring to the table. So, go out and find YOUR own rhythm, YOUR own beat, and create such a beautiful song that it leaves every person you meet humming the tune.

Change Ya Mindset Change Ya Life

Hope is stronger than fear...strengthen it and watch your fears dwindle

Hope is such a strong and proven commodity that it doesn't get the recognition it deserves. The depths of hope in tomorrow will never diminish. Hope is the only thing left standing when everything else seems to walk out. Life is full of curve balls. The good news is that it doesn't matter how bad you swing and miss...You always get another at-bat. Hope provides an array of energy that sparks the action behind solving each trial and tribulation that we may endure. It's easy to give up. It's easy to think and accept things for the way they are. When life is beating you down...That's when the hope begins to arrive. Deep down, it sits & hovers like a still water. Next time you feel a rush to give up...I dare you to look up. Witness the gleam within the sky...because that's the hope you're looking for. You have to believe in the unseen to get out of the hole. So sit back, focus and knock the next curve ball out of the park.

Change Ya Mindset Change Ya Life

Invest in the struggle...it's the only way you get out

For too often, people view struggle as a problem, yet, our struggles are not here to punish us, but to show us something. Everything has its purpose and the good will shine through the struggle. It may not be today, tomorrow, a week, a month or even a year from now, but it will shine. Everything from loss, death, abuse, homelessness, being poor, being taken advantage of...everything that you can imagine is all a part of something that is bigger than yourself and will be used for the greater good towards you as a person. Each day I challenge you to have some trust in yourself, view struggle as a gift, and continue to ride the wave that it's presenting. Even if you get knocked off while riding you'll still be able to enjoy the water. It might be the refreshing moment that you need to take the next step.

Change Ya Mindset Change Ya Life

Every chapter should have something new, if not, re-evaluate your daily habits

You control the pen to dictate what is written within your life. You always have the opportunity to control the narrative. With every experience something new should be on the horizon. Examine your habits within your routine that deals with your physical, mental, emotional and spiritual well being. Each part is so crucial to who you are and needs to be challenged; it needs to be approached with wanting & craving the next level. Don't get comfortable and settle for mediocrity. You are meant for bigger. I would hope that you see the greatness that's waiting to be unleashed. In 1900, with only 3 years of high school education, Orville and Wilbur Wright set out to invent the first airplane. By 1903 they had successfully achieved their goal. Do you think they settled? They didn't and continued to develop their craft with things that are still used today...If they didn't settle why should you? Think about it. It's your turn to fly.

Change Ya Mindset Change Ya Life

When your why is greater than everything else than the difficult things seem to carry less value

Imagine if we didn't allow life to dictate our dreams. If we were so focused on achieving our dreams that we were too stubborn to give up. It takes a lot of courage to come back every single day after being knocked down. But that's what makes it worth it. When you envision your dreams meeting its purpose then the dream comes to life. Everybody has a "why" and if you don't, it's time to discover it. Your "why" is the reason you get up and fight everyday. Don't let anyone or anything disrupt that dream. At the end of the day it's not about you...it's bigger. One of the best examples I can give: you resemble a puzzle piece; when looking at the box full of pieces each piece seems insignificant, but when the puzzle is complete each piece has its purpose. The world needs you and your gifts. You have purpose, so, place your "why" at the forefront. The puzzle is incomplete without you.

Change Ya Mindset Change Ya Life

The greatest thing about you can't be measured...And that scares people

The greatest thing about us as an individual is the fact that we all are different and the world needs all of us to make it what it is. People who are afraid or hate on you is because they don't understand you, what you do or how you do it. They can't do what you do and it creates fear and jealousy. That's there issue, not yours. You have to keep in mind, no one can diminish your value. No one can take away the things that make you great. Those are yours to have, keep and share. Stop wasting your energy on other people's opinions and the negativity they throw at you. Think of how awesome it is that no one in this world can do what you do and how you do it. It's time for you to introduce yourself to the world. Turn your volume up...It's time to be heard.

Change Ya Mindset Change Ya Life

Your words should never be ahead of your actions

It seems to be a common theme in our society that people like to bark (verbally tell people their plans and hype themselves up) and have no bite to back it up (no action, no motivation, no energy, no focus, no effort towards anything they talk about). We spend too much time comparing ourselves to others and not enough time focusing on DOING. Compete with self and challenge the unseen. It will force and produce an issue of impact with those around you. If you're impacting lives then you're succeeding. That impact will carry on to all those people that they know. It becomes a Domino effect. Your legacy is built off impact. Not how you hype yourself up. We live in a generation now where the best things in life are unexpected. So, for now keep your songs under-wraps and let the surprise of a midnight album release shock the world...For the better.

Change Ya Mindset Change Ya Life

People don't need to be fixed. They aren't broken...They just need to be reshaped

Imagine if we approached situations with a mindset that things don't need to be fixed. People weren't born broken, they just have had a hard road and need to be reshaped in order to get back on track. The term broken leaves such a bad stigma that unfairly places judgment on people, which in turn, makes it harder to overcome. With a different view, think about how much more impact could be accomplished. The possibilities are endless. It all starts with us investing in self so we can achieve a perspective to help and impact those we cross paths with. We all have the ability to grow, learn and propel forward. We all have the ability to make a difference. We all have the ability to impact. So, at the end of the day we all are a can of silly putty...We just need to be reworked sometimes so that our greatness can be fully on display.

Change Ya Mindset Change Ya Life

Your perspective is shaped by what you're hungry for

Your ability to view things in a different manner is vital. Feed your mind positive or neutral content. That will condition your mind to reshape itself into leaning on those pieces of content during difficult/different situations. It takes a ton of courage and trust to look yourself in the mirror and know changes need to be made. The best way to start is to start...Books, videos, conversations with others, music, writing...Etc. Everyone will get their perspectives from different avenues. Seeking and craving different views on situations will be the best decision you could ever make. Remove the horrible nutrition that is being consumed. It's time to strip away the negative, cut the calories and become hungry again...For the better.

Change Ya Mindset Change Ya Life

Stay humble and let your passion speak for you

The loudest person in the room isn't the one to learn from. It's the one who observes & learns. You have a gift and when you let your passion speak for you it creates a greater impact than any words expressed. Staying humble allows you to stay hungry which will challenge you to never settle and push forward. Letting your passion speak will allow your actions to do the talking., It will allow you to stay within the moment and continue to create without missing a beat. Gloating takes away from the action. Set the standard for the next while still creating your own. You hold the paintbrush. Don't ruin the vision by dumping paint on the beautiful image. Continue to add an array of colors to fit the picture. Without even realizing it, you have a wide range of fans who can't take their eyes off of it.

Forgive. Not for them. For you, and watch the power they have on your mind and heart disappear.

Forgiveness is the strongest thing you could do in your life. When people hurt you, disrespect you, take advantage of you, we often dwell on those people and situations. When you dwell you leave the door open for those people to control your thoughts. That power is killing your spirit. Have courage to forgive those who have hurt you & you will quickly notice a weight being lifted and how much room in your mind it creates. You owe it to yourself to give yourself the best opportunity to live the life you were meant to live. Don't let the past destroy you. Vent, iron out your thoughts, take away the good from the situation and move forward. Take the power back. It's time to be a symbol of true strength. It's time to take back the control of the pen and write your story.

Change Ya Mindset Change Ya Life

Troubles and trials are not meant to punish us but to awaken us to slow down and create focus on the small details that make a huge difference

Every day brings something new. Life throws punches. When you get punched in the face your focus should shift from shock to purpose. Punches are meant to slow us down in life, we often get so carried away and wrapped up in our own worlds that we lose sight of the important things that matter the most. It's a wake up call, so, pick up the phone and re-focus on the small details of life. Those small details are going to take you to the next level in anything that you do and will help you continue to climb. You're going to be in a 12 round fight when it comes to life and it will feel as if your hands are tied behind your back and you can't punch back. Embrace the fight and get ready to go the distance because that is going to put you on the path to better things. Once you free your mind from imaginary handcuffs...Your 1-2 combo will be something that nobody can beat.

Change Ya Mindset Change Ya Life

The clarity of empty triggers untapped creativity

Empty provides a canvas with free reign to create. At any given moment, you can become and pursue anything that you want. Make a decision to go after it. Feeling empty is common, a lot more common than people realize, but that doesn't give you the reason to make excuses and give up. The emptiness is the building block that you need to turn your life around. It's a necessity to challenge us in all aspects. The emptiness will allow your mind to navigate down avenues that you never even imagined. The emptiness provides us to reach a level within that helps us tap into unknown potential and creativity that we didn't even know we possessed. Through that navigation you'll discover such greatness that you'll spark a permanent motivation to overcome. Stop living in an empty room. You're meant to explore & the world is waiting to see what you discover.

Change Ya Mindset Change Ya Life

Change Ya Mindset Change Ya Life

To break the mold it sparks common things done in an uncommon manner

Getting ahead in life and impacting lives can be accomplished by doing common things. Adding your own flare and flavor is the game changer. It shows that you are here but prepared to impact beyond the moment. It allows you to showcase who you are to the world. It allows you to show that your experiences haven't destroyed you but built you up. Get people's attention and do common things in an uncommon manner. People are used to the same old things that they have an oversight of what's in front of them. So, instead of hiding from the world I think it's time you break the mold. I think it's time you peel when everyone else slices. I think it's time your actions spark the next great mind and your impact transcends generations. I think it's time you fly above the clouds while everyone else hovers over the city.

You have a daily FEE...Life doesn't owe you. So give your focus, energy and effort and watch your greatness appear

Each day comes with opportunity but our world let's it's selfish nature take over and our vision gets blurred. Harsh reality...Life doesn't owe you anything. Everything you get you earn by giving. Give focus, your focus to your loved ones and dreams. Give energy, high energy will naturally attract better circumstances and people, you won't have to force anything, people and opportunities will present themselves. Give full effort, people are taking notice. You have full control and these three things speak volumes without having to say a word. Life doesn't owe you, YOU OWE LIFE a daily FEE...(F)ocus, (E)nergy, (E)ffort. Start giving back to life and your greatness will be hard to ignore. It's time to be different. It's hard to dismiss a person who gives out FEE's rather than collects them.

Change Ya Mindset Change Ya Life

The biggest limitation is put on you by YOU...So turn your fear into food and feed your goals

A person you see every single day of life is yourself. That means you have the ultimate control over what happens to you. Only you, can stop you. Stop putting limitations on yourself. Stop feeding yourself lies about your abilities. Stop being afraid to take chances. Stop being afraid to be great. Start thinking outside the box that you've placed yourself in. One of the worst things in the world is untapped potential, your goal should be to use every once of it before you leave this earth. It's time to start starving your fears. Your fears are a unique collection that will provide a drive within that will push you towards something bigger. It's time to turn those fears into food and fuel your goals. You've been starving the wrong things in life...It's time to load your plate up and eat.

Change Ya Mindset Change Ya Life

Harness the storm within and it'll produce a quiet confidence that echoes a big impact

Bull riding...As you watch, the moments leading up are a bowl of mixed emotions. It's 8 seconds full of nervousness, excitement, and anxiousness. You get to see a rush of emotions play out in real life. They harness the bull and walk it into the cage, the bull rider straps in, gives the nod, and BOOM...It happens. Similar to life's storms. The storm has every emotion you can imagine within it. Instead of being consumed by the storm, harness it and use those emotions for a greater good. Imagine if you harness all those emotions and at the right time...BOOM, it happens. You unleash all of those emotions into a quiet confidence that leads you down a better path. It gets you back on track and gives you the hope that you need. Next time you feel overwhelmed, strap in, hang on, and visualize 8 seconds...It's one great ride.

Tears are good. Let it out. You find strength within the tears and the knowledge that you can go another round and you got more punches to throw.

Majority of people bottle things up until you have no other choice but to let them out, more times than not, in a negative manner. What if you allowed yourself to express yourself with a greater good in mind. Acknowledge your emotions and express them in a positive manner. Allow yourself an opportunity to discover the greater good a lot sooner. I view tears as an outlet that lets us flow from sadness to hope. The process in between is what makes the end of the river, worth the wait. Next time you want to hold back tears...Don't. They are the gateway to something special. They allow your soul to cleanse. They allow your mind to release pressure. Tears are a gift that have their place. Stop holding yourself back, unleash the tears & find the freedom you're looking for in order to continue the fight. Allow those cuffs to come off and equip yourself with the strength that is hidden within each drop.

Change Ya Mindset Change Ya Life

If we fail to tap into the depths of who we are, what we are capable of, in all aspects. Then we are failing at using the gift to the utmost.

Everyone has a gift. As you walk through life, most of you just walk and don't tap into who you are. If you fail to tap into yourself you risk the chance of never discovering what you are truly meant to do. It's a process but has meaning. Struggle provides an opportunity to look at things in a global view. Struggle provides a chance for true clarity. You have to challenge yourself to get there. Think about how important the trickle effect is for your life. You and your gifts matter. What you do matters and a greater good is waiting. Someone is counting on you. Start tapping into your full potential and let the world know that you're here. You'd be surprised what happens when you truly open your eyes. The possibilities are endless. Go change your life for the better and spark the explosion that creates the avenue you're meant to travel down.

3 guarantees in life...The light shines, the darkness hovers, and we always have the choice between the two.

At the end of the day it's about where we choose to put forth our focus. Everyone has a choice. See the light or let the darkness consume you. If you find yourself consumed by the darkness the people you surround yourself with have the keys to open up your mind to different perspectives. One view will lead you down a dead end road. Experience different perspectives and gain a wealth of enjoyment, appreciation, and insight that will produce opportunities that lead to impact. Feed yourself different resources and enhance your ability to see the light and impact those around you. At the end of the day choose to put forth your focus on something that will alter your view for the better. Refuse to believe in the map that leads you to road blocks. Live life the way it's meant to be lived. The lights always there to guide you. All it takes is a flip of a switch and the road in front of you becomes everything you could imagine.

Change Ya Mindset Change Ya Life

Beautiful chaos foreshadows mere seconds of pure joy. Building blocks to not only survive the storm but come out with a sense of accomplishment

The storm is not about the storm in itself...It's about something bigger. The storm is purely what happens between the beautiful chaos and the sunshine on the other side. It takes focus, but you can recognize the beauty that the storm possess. Merely surviving will be needed but YOU ARE equipped to do so. Throughout the storm that beauty that you discovered will point you in different directions that will provide different opportunities. At the end of the day, the storm is a blessing and will be so vital to your growth and development. Your storm(s) have purpose, there is nothing in life that happens just because. Pure joy is on the other side and waiting. Change your mindset. A beautiful rainbow with an array of colors is a lot closer to appearing than you think. Let's look deeper into the storm...It's time to see the colors that show you the true meaning of life.

Change Ya Mindset Change Ya Life

Stop putting pleasure before purpose. Attain discipline and watch your grind open up variety within opportunity.

Our world is consumed by immediate results and false perceptions of reality. Anyone who ever achieved on a great level put forth so much time and effort before reaching any sort of pleasure. The one thing that separates the GREATS from the majority is their DISCIPLINE. Once they locked in, their grind took them to new levels. No matter how they were viewed or if they were understood, the grind and discipline opened the doors. If you're only goal is the outcome...Then you're missing the gifts in between. Great growth lies within the experience. It will allow you to shift your mindset, not only to succeed, but to pass on the blueprint to the next for impact. So, stand off to the side...You're not meant to be a part of the crowd...You're built to be the one they pay attention to.

Change Ya Mindset Change Ya Life

Don't run from your problems. Attack them full force & realize you're fighting for the person in the mirror...And beyond what's looking back at you.

Look in the mirror. You see what's staring back at you? It's life...It's your past...And it's your future. Everyone goes through problems and the only difference between anybody is the fact that some choose to fight. Fight for yourself. Fight for your family and friends. Fight with your past in mind but your future at the forefront of it all. You have to stop running away and start taking that strength you possess deep down and start fightin back. You're not meant to just live and let things happen. You have more control than you think you do. Let's start controlling the narrative. Stand up for yourself. Realize that what's looking back at you in the mirror is going to do something great. If you can't see what's beyond the mirror than a haymaker will be headed your way and you won't be able to get up. Each year of life is a new round and it's time to start throwing life that 1-2 combo that nobody can beat. So pair some faith with some hard work and watch the score of the fight turn into your favor.

Life is meant to be lived in moments. Imagine if we lived unmasked...Moments would never perish and we'd experience it in a way that would allow them to last as if they never ended.

Living life is truly special. It's amazing the moments you get to experience. How often do we live a life where you are so preoccupied by the thoughts of others that it takes away from the moments. It takes away from the experience. Flip the script, what would happen if you took off the masks that you wear to impress people and left them on the side of the road? What if you stopped worrying about the thoughts of others and just lived. Imagine how many more moments you'd fully get to experience and enjoy, which in turn, would add so many more memories to your collection that you can carry with you the rest of your life. Those added moments turn into stories, those stories turn into impact, and that impact turns into a full life that was lived to the utmost. It's time to undo the mask. It's time to leave the fear and doubt behind. Pull over, drop the mask and experience more of the world to the fullest.

Change Ya Mindset Change Ya Life

Passion exceeds acknowledgment. Stay hungry. Stay humble. Life is bigger than one's ego.

When passion leads acknowledgment seems secondary. Your passion has great value that goes unnoticed because our world has a habit of killing it at the roots. When passion leads, it's allowed an opportunity to breathe, grow, expand, impact, and leave a lasting mark on those you come in contact with. Making sure you get noticed is wasted energy. All of that takes care of itself. Don't allow success to diminish your hunger. Never settle and never be satisfied with what you did yesterday. Strive for more every day. Stay humble. Never let your past or current success drive you down an empty path. Tough reality...Life is not about you...But it is about who you impact. Your ego can be used for good when it's pointed in the right direction and your life will be immensely better. Stay Humble, Stay Hungry, and get your GPS out. Your ego and overall life are depending on it.

Change Ya Mindset Change Ya Life

Let us not listen but hear for substance...If you put forth effort you'll notice the difference.

There's a difference between listening to someone and actually hearing them. When people listen they are not fully focused on what is being said, rather, they are more concerned with their response. When someone actually takes the time to hear someone they have their full focus on what is being said to them. They are fully invested and want to understand. When someone is hearing what is said they are fully tuned in and able to give a response that is geared towards helping, if needed. Too many people only listen because they are so wrapped up in their own worlds that they fail the person talking to them. They are placing their own agendas above the person speaking. Let us hear for substance and watch how much impact we can create on a daily basis. Which in turn will produce an effect like non-other. It's truly amazing when we invest in one another and how the possibilities become endless.

Change Ya Mindset Change Ya Life

Your word choice to yourself and others affects beyond the current moment.

Your words have great power. I can guarantee that you've been on the wrong side of someone projecting an array of words on you and captivating a hold on your mind and actions moving forward. You have the power to uplift and inspire merely by your words with what you say and how you say it. If you speak with energy, passion and genuine intent when you talk then your words are going to spark the next person to go create the next great thing our world needs. You all have a gift and conversation can highlight those gifts. Be an outlet and a resource to one another. Truly invest and spark the next great mind. While watching one another develop you develop and, in turn, the beauty of the world develops. It all starts with your word choice. Instead of cutting the legs out from each other with a lack of consciousness, let's hone in, and provide each other with a different pair of shoes to walk in and chase our dreams.

Change Ya Mindset Change Ya Life

The unreasonable person makes the greatest progress because they don't ever allow themselves to fall into the trap of reality. Think outside the box...Watch greatness appear.

Reality will try to suck the passion out of you. Reality will try to turn you into something that you hate. You need to use all the strength you possess. All the stubborn nature. All the "crazy" that might be within you and use it to push it towards who you want to be, what you want to do and what you want to accomplish. You're capable of a lot more than reality tells you. You're meant to do bigger things than what reality says and it's time to start acting like it. It's time to be unreasonable with your life. If the joy is missing then it's time to make a change. Go after something that you've been told, your whole life, that you're not good enough for. It's time to dig deep. Pull that unreasonable person out and use it to your advantage. You're meant to be great. Block out reality and go after what you want. Choose yourself, choose peace of mind, choose the vision that you had when you were a kid, and bring that vision to life. Dreams to reality...it's not as crazy as you might think.

Change Ya Mindset Change Ya Life

Gratitude will take you places that your mind can't even imagine.

Gratitude is one of the greatest things in our world that is expressed. Said often, but it's over looked. We get the opportunity to live, to improve our lives, to help others, to participate in a variety of different things. Yet, we often dwell on the bad, on the struggle, and on the obstacles far too much that we overlook the good. Someone always has it worse than what we appear of our lives to be. Yet, there is someone out there who does have it worse who also has a better mindset and approach to their situation. Put forth so much focus on being grateful for not only what you have but for what you've been through. Your past has shaped you and it has prepared you for what's to come. The strength lies within the struggle. Once you realize that showing gratitude for your past and present opens the door to opportunity then the vision of your future begins to appear through the haze. Your life isn't meant to be lived within smog so let gratitude clear the air.

Change Ya Mindset Change Ya Life

Your ability to reflect on the greater good in mind will take you miles ahead of the next.

Never let struggle consume you. Never let what appears to be the downfall of your life ruin your life. There is a purpose for everything that you go through. That statement is hard to hear and hard to grasp at times because you can't understand why things have happened or why they are happening the way that they are. You always have a choice to either live in the past, continue to focus on things that are already done, over with and let them consume you into your present. Or, you can choose the latter, give forth your focus in other areas that will propel you to the next great thing that is waiting for you. Greatness and opportunity are waiting for you to get out of the past and push forward...That is the only way the door opens. It's time to get out of the haunted past that scares you from the future. My advice, shut the door to the past. Pick up a hammer, walk to the door of your future and start beating it down. Don't just open it. Break it so there's no barrier for what's waiting for you.

Change Ya Mindset Change Ya Life

Change Ya Mindset Change Ya Life

It's amazing what happens when you realize what you owe yourself...And then you start grinding like it.

You have the power to change anything at any time. Look at what's in front of you and realize that better is on the horizon. Great things await behind the door and we are the only ones who possess the key. Stop thinking you're not worthy of something great in your life. Stop letting comparison be the thief of life. Stop letting people tell you that you're average and that you always will be. Nobody was born for mediocrity and yet you allow outside influences to control your path...Why? You have a choice, every morning when you wake up to go attack the day with passion and energy. Two things that are the most contagious qualities in the world. You have the ability to push beyond the comparisons. It's time you realize you're destined for something above the opinions of others. Stop listening and start GRINDING. It's amazing what hard work will produce. It's amazing what energy and passion will produce. It's amazing what a strong WILL will produce. You have the power at your fingertips. Remember, you possess the key to greatness...I suggest you use it.

Your ability to believe in the unseen and chase it will take you beyond anything tangible.

Everything takes time and patience, but once you find your groove, everything seems to fall into place. Your ability to believe in those moments are what is crucial in your development as a person. If you can train your mind to believe through the dark days, the homeless nights, the abuse, the missed meals, the lack of money in the bank account. If you can train your mind to flip the script and see the beauty within the struggle and believe that better days, that are full of great experiences and opportunities, are on the horizon then you will be set-up on a path that puts any other avenue to shame. Put forth focus on one thing at a time, give it your absolute everything within yourself, and things will begin to turn around. Create a domino effect for yourself and check things off your list. It's time to believe in yourself beyond what you see and put forth a vision that will come to life.

Stop waiting for someone else to cook your food. Get in the kitchen and stop depending on those who only steal your ingredients

You possess everything you need to go after what you want. Stop letting society tell you that you aren't special, that you aren't talented, that the timing isn't right. Those are all lies that are fed to you. Shift your eyes and ears to the positivity and encouragement that gets drowned out. You're meant to live above the hate and you're meant to out grow the people around you that bring you down. Your circle should be one that challenges you and raises you to a new level. Not people who steal your peace of mind, motivation and drive. The balls in your court. Handle it with care and once you see your opening take it. Life's too short to never shoot.

Change Ya Mindset Change Ya Life

Investment in yourself with the intentions of investing in others to create a trickle effect impact that transcends generations

A ton of people think that they aren't worthy. They believe that life is meant to be lived one way because of how things have been presented to them through other's thoughts and opinions. They allow others to control their view of self. Start ignoring the outside noise and invest in self, commit to self, and then proceed to invest in others. You leave your mark on this world with the type of impact that you create. Your impact will trigger an explosion that destroys obstacles and limitations that have been placed on ourselves and others. It's time to build up yourself...To build up others. Legacy lives forever. You are a construction worker that has plenty of business lined up. So grab your hard hat, your payment for you work will be worth more than any amount of money you can imagine...Your name will live on forever.

Change Ya Mindset Change Ya Life

The X-factor will always be your gift & your passion...It's invaluable.

Nobody else does what you do in the way you do it. We all get presented with different gifts and a different way of presenting them to the world. That doesn't mean you have to act all high and mighty but it does give you reassurance that what you do and how you do it will be valued because you're the only one who does it in that particular fashion. Your style and flavor won't be everyone's cup of tea and that is perfectly okay. Hang your hat on impact. If people who don't approve or see value in what you do then they are failing to see the impact you're creating. That isn't your problem but theirs. You always need to, no matter what gets thrown your way, continue to focus on the impact that you're creating. Forget those who fail to see your value of what you do and how you do it. Those people will be at the base steps of the ladder and try to climb and catch you. That's okay...You're not going in that direction anyways.

Change Ya Mindset Change Ya Life

Failure is the gateway to reflection. Reflection is the gateway to discovery. Discovery is the gateway to YOUR path of success

Failure is a must. It provides so many opportunities that leads to reflection...Leads to discovery...That will lead to your path of impact and success. You need to relish failure. It will be the best thing that ever happens to you. The opportunity to learn outweighs all. No one has ever came into this world and been successful at everything. Failure is all a part of the process. Don't get discouraged that things are not happening right away or in the time frame that you believe they should happen. Hard work...Failure...Hard work...Failure....You need to repeat this process for as long as it takes. You need to carry such a strong belief in yourself and pair it with a strength to continue with the process that it turns your failures into the success you crave. Failure is the mother of all successes, it's time to show failure the love it deserves...

Change Ya Mindset Change Ya Life

The way you see yourself dictates your value. Raise your level of self and grind for what you're meant to be

Every day you need to view yourself as a person of value. You are a person who has more value than can be expressed in any form. What you bring to the table is needed in this world and if you don't think so then our world is missing out on such an impactful piece. The way you see yourself will attract opportunities based off pure presence. Once you recognize your value you walk around with confidence that isn't loud, but more so, a quiet swagger that people take notice of. Your vibe when you walk into any room will announce itself without any words having to be spoken. I challenge you to raise your level of self. Look at yourself differently and work for what you've always wanted. Once you see your value the spark triggers and it'll be hard for anyone to put out.

Change Ya Mindset Change Ya Life

Your structure is the foundation, yet, your mindset triggers the work ethic to elevate you to a different height.

Your mindset. Your approach. Is what will separate you from the rest of the crowd. You build your foundation from the ground up and your mindset is what takes you over the top. You don't play the victim role but confront your problems head on, take accountability, and look for different ways to adjust to what life is throwing at you. You must work and believe in a fashion that is different from the majority around you or what you witness. Life is hard but bowing down to life is never an option. There is good in all we go through. Life will throw you curveballs but if you prepare yourself to sit back and wait...Your patience and approach will lead you towards hitting the ball out of the park.

Change Ya Mindset Change Ya Life

You don't belong in a box. Relish the choice to be different. Your style will create something that's never been seen before...

Never settle. You deserve to be great and to showcase that greatness to the world. The perceptions of others and the box they may place you in has no reflection of you and every bit of a reflection of them. You are different, we all are, and you have to value that. The ways you are different are the exact reasons why you're going to impact this world beyond measure. You can't let the small minds of the world knock you down and win. You have to stay the course. Continue to evolve and stay true to who you are. Harsh reality, there will always be people who are going to knock you down when they are unfamiliar with the way you do things. There's not one way to do things and when others come in and produce with a different strategy it scares people. Don't let other people's fears and insecurities diminish your value and purpose. It's time for you to set the standard. It's time for you to raise the stakes and force the issue on everyone else. It's time for you honor the fact that your own style will change the world.

Change Ya Mindset Change Ya Life

Your current situation has no correlation with your future. Struggle enhances the vision. Look deep into traffic. Find the avenues that most think are dead ends.

Trust yourself enough to realize that your current life will not be the way it ends. There will be more things that happen and occur that will change your mindset. Be open to the fact that opportunities will be disguised as struggle and that for you to overcome your current situation you have to train your mind to believe in the unseen. It won't be right square in front of you but that doesn't mean you give up. It takes a unique person to look at the side roads and see a way out...You are that unique person. It's time to tap in to who you are on a deeper level and locate that strength and creativity to get out of the hole you may be in. Struggle is your way out and it's time to use it as a windshield wiper...Your ability to see ahead needs it.

Change Ya Mindset Change Ya Life

Change Ya Mindset Change Ya Life

Your failures provides an opportunity for improvement beyond the surface. Failure doesn't define you, yet, surrendering will...

Failure is inevitable. How we respond to that failure is always in our hands. Failure produces such great growth and opportunities to reflect. The surface of our world creates such an unrealistic expectation that failure seems to be a downfall, yet, it is the exact thing that our journey's need. Failure and how we react is a direct reflection on how our impact and success will shape. Failure is going to slap you in the face but that doesn't mean you should give up. Failure will never define you but if you surrender then you are letting those voices, who are expecting you to fail and give up, win. You're letting outside sources raise the volume and speak negativity into existence. It's time to fight back. It's time to learn. It's time to grow. You're not a one hit wonder...You're built for multi-platinum success.

Impossible is the greatest setup to achieve greatness. Raise your grind and watch impossible turn into common.

The term "impossible" is for those people who lack the understanding that anything can be achieved with a great work ethic and faith. Believing in self and in something bigger than yourself will take you to a different level of perspective and will produce. Stop letting other people tell you, "it's impossible for you to go do what you want to do...You're not built for that." Impossible is for small minded people who lack the understanding of the bigger picture. All it takes is a spark and a stubborn nature. Don't let others place their limitations and insecurities on you. It's your life and it's your time to rise above their altitude of thinking. So hop on the plane to possible and enjoy the view.

Change Ya Mindset Change Ya Life

Once you realize the way you view the world is to your advantage. That will be the moment you go attack mode. Don't feel pressure, yet, flip the script and push the pace.

There will be people who don't agree with how you do things. Your approach won't be acceptable simply because it is different than the "norm." Your style, flare and flavor will scare people. Don't ever let others opinions, agendas or insecurities take away from who you are, what you do, and how you do it. Embrace the reactions from others and realize everything that you are is what makes you special and how you impact the lives around you. Flip the script on this world and push the pace. You are capable of becoming the best fast break that the world has ever seen. You are unstoppable once you realize that your style and flavor is just what this world is missing...Go change the game and set the next standard for those who come behind you.

Change Ya Mindset Change Ya Life

Don't let struggle interrupt the vision

Struggle will be the best thing to ever happen to you. It will provide so much opportunity and clarity. It will be the gateway to where you want to go and who you want to be.. If you fully immerse yourself in the struggle. Don't run from it and don't deny that it's happening. If you run and deny it the vision gets blurry and the time for it to come to fruition becomes delayed. It's time to go attack mode on your struggle. Struggle doesn't own you. No time for a pity party. No time to be a victim. It's time to pick up your head, puff out your chest, and let it be known that you run the block. Struggle will try to break into your home. It's time to kick it to the curb and take your place of peace back.

Change Ya Mindset Change Ya Life

Change is waiting. Have the courage and choose a life of pursuit.

Everything starts with a choice. Every day when you wake up you have a choice to be great. It doesn't matter what has happened to you in the past, present, or future. It all comes back to you and your mindset. If choose to not let others opinions or judgments affect you then your life will instantly become better. If you choose to act with love over hate, give instead of take, attack instead of settle then your life will instantly improve tremendously. You control the narrative and don't let anyone ever tell you different. It's your life and it's time to start acting like it. So have the courage to make the choice to create the change. Change ya mindset change ya life and watch dreams turn into reality.

Change Ya Mindset Change Ya Life

THANK YOU!

First and foremost I want to thank my parents for the continued love and support through this stretch of trials and tribulations. You instilled in me a long time ago how our last name rings an immeasurable amount of strength with each letter. It's what gives me the energy to keep going with early mornings and late nights. Thank you for never giving up on me.

Secondly, a special thank you to my big brother Josh, without hesitation he stepped up to be the protector and stable foundation while the roller coaster took off within a blink of an eye. I wouldn't be where I am today if it wasn't for you...thank you for seeing something in me that I didn't see in myself. Thank you for the help with food, clothes, a place to put my feet up and the push I need to chase something bigger than myself.

Hayley J Peterson, she made a joke one day to name the book after her, which then got my mind working, so I used her initials & it prompted the title - Harmony Joins Perspective. She also created the cover and her story has inspired me well beyond the moment she told me it. Thank you kid for allowing me to be a part of your journey! Keep using your gift to the fullest!

Thank you to every single kid I've had the blessing of being a mentor, educator and/or coach to. The amount of creativity and juice that you spark in me can't be expressed enough. Humbled and Honored to be a part of the process and the journey for each and every single one of you. Never forget that each of you has a gift, let's work together to discover it, use it, and impact this world...LEAVE YOUR MARK!

An incredibly HUGE shoutout to Cale & Angelique Henderson and Jeff & Sally Guy. You four have literally helped a kid who was projected to never amount to anything introduce himself to the world in a very unique way. Your selfless actions of opening up your homes gave me a sense of comfort and stability; it will never be forgotten. These words won't bring justice to what your actions have meant to me. From the bottom of my heart thank you for everything.

Lastly, a very special thank you to John Shaffer. A conversation back in December of 2018 sparked this whole process. He planted the seed of sharing my story with the world. He's an incredibly gifted person who is impacting this world in his own right. He started from the bottom to create his own media agency (nvzn). He's impacting the world with each piece of content he puts out. Thank you for the push little brother. This is just the start and I'm excited for what the future holds for the both of us.

Thank you to everyone along my journey. You've impacted and inspired me more than you can imagine. Each day is an opportunity for all of us to get better and for all of us to succeed. No jealousy, envy or selfishness...ONLY IMPACT! THANK YOU ALL!